Garfield's Almost-as-Great-as-Pizza Guide to TECHNOLOGY

Rebecca E. Hirsch

Garfield created by JIM DAVIS

LERNER PUBLICATIONS ◆ MINNEAPOLIS

In memory of my mother-in-law, Alice Hirsch

Visit Garfield online at https://www.garfield.com

Lerner Publications Company
A division of Lerner Publishing Group, Inc.
241 First Avenue North
Minneapolis, MN 55401 USA

For reading levels and more information, look up this title at www.lernerbooks.com.

Main body text set in Neo Sans Std 13/20.
Typeface provided by Monotype Typography.

Library of Congress Cataloging-in-Publication Data

Names: Hirsch, Rebecca E., author.
Title: Garfield's almost-as-great-as-pizza guide to technology / Rebecca E. Hirsch.
Other titles: Almost as-great-as-pizza guide to technology
Description: Minneapolis : Lerner Publications, [2020] | Series: Garfield's fat cat guide to STEM breakthroughs | Audience: Ages 7-11. | Audience: Grades 4 to 6. | Includes bibliographical references and index.
Identifiers: LCCN 2018044368 (print) | LCCN 2018046017 (ebook) | ISBN 9781541561908 (eb pdf) | ISBN 9781541546394 (lib. bdg.)
Subjects: LCSH: Technology—History—Juvenile literature. | Inventions—History— Juvenile literature. | Davis, Jim, 1945 July 28- Garfield—Juvenile literature.
Classification: LCC T15 (ebook) | LCC T15 .H56 2020 (print) | DDC 609—dc23

LC record available at https://lccn.loc.gov/2018044368

Manufactured in the United States of America
1-45568-41277-12/28/2018

Contents

The First Tools

A long time ago, our ancient ancestors used tools for hunting and cooking. The first tools were stone tools. They were made by striking round pieces of stone with another stone to make them sharper.

The oldest stone tools are 3.3 million years old. They were discovered poking out of the ground in Africa. There were scars along the edges of the stones. The scars show that someone had chipped away at the edges. The tools may have been used to cut meat.

Early American Indians also carved objects out of stone, such as these arrowheads.

Fire

Sometime in the distant past, ancient people began to use fire. Early people had witnessed natural fire from lightning strikes. Fire gave people light and warmth as well as a way to cook food.

HOW ABOUT SOME HOT DOGS AND MARSHMALLOWS WITH THAT FIRE?

Most people use fire for recreation these days, but our early ancestors used it for survival.

But when did people learn how to control fire? The oldest evidence shows people were using fire one million years ago. Researchers discovered wood ash and charred animal bones inside a large cave. The burned remains were found in Wonderwerk Cave in South Africa.

The Wheel

More than five thousand years ago, people invented the wheel. Wheels don't exist in nature. They are a human invention. A wheel is a disc that turns on an axle.

THIS IS HOW I ROLL!

Wheels are one of humankind's earliest inventions.

The first wheels were created in Mesopotamia, part of modern-day Iraq. Potters used them to make clay pots. About three hundred years later, the era of transportation got rolling. People put wheels on carts. These carts had two or four wheels and were pulled by horses. Wheeled carts soon spread to other parts of the world.

Timekeeping

About five thousand years ago, Egyptian astronomers invented a way to tell time using the movement of the sun. They built tall towers, which showed the passage of time with a moving shadow. Later, they built sundials, which marked the time by a shadow cast on markers. But those early clocks didn't work when the sun wasn't shining.

IS IT NAPTIME YET?

Stone sundials were once the most reliable way to keep time.

Egyptians later invented water clocks. These clocks measured time by water dripping from a container at a constant rate. Markings on the container measured the passage of time. In the thirteenth century, modern clocks were invented. They used the swinging of a pendulum to measure time.

The Printing Press

Before printing, every book had to be written by hand. In the ninth century, Chinese monks invented ways to print books. They carved characters and pictures on wood. When the inked wood was pressed against paper, the characters were printed on the paper. In the eleventh century, Chinese inventor Pi Sheng made movable type. He put single characters on small clay blocks. The blocks could be used and reused.

Around 1450 Johannes Gutenberg of Germany invented the printing press. The wooden machine had metal movable type. With Gutenberg's machine, books could be printed easily and cheaply.

Johannes Gutenberg

13

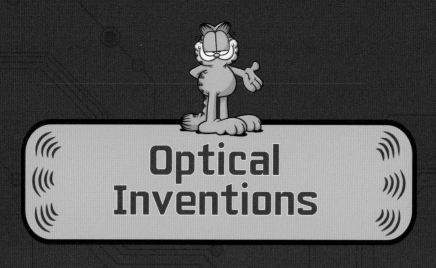

Optical Inventions

Since the first century, people knew that glass bends light rays. In the tenth century, Arab scientist Ibn al-Haytham from modern Iraq explained how people see. He realized that we see objects because light bounces off an object to our eyes. He is called the father of modern optics.

An early telescope

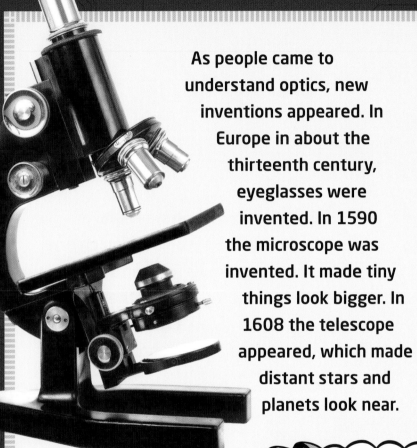

As people came to understand optics, new inventions appeared. In Europe in about the thirteenth century, eyeglasses were invented. In 1590 the microscope was invented. It made tiny things look bigger. In 1608 the telescope appeared, which made distant stars and planets look near.

Microscopes help scientists get a close-up view of objects.

WELL, THAT CLEARS THINGS UP!

Engine Evolution

In 1860 Belgian inventor Étienne Lenoir invented the first internal combustion engine. It was lighter and more powerful than steam engines, which were widely used at the time. His engine burned fuel inside a chamber. The energy released pushed a piston up and down in a cylinder.

POOKY AND I PREFER PEDAL POWER

Internal combustion engines power many modern-day cars and trucks.

Two years later, Lenoir attached his engine to a wagon and made a 6-mile (10 km) road trip. Then he used it to power a motorboat.

The internal combustion engine changed transportation forever. These engines power cars, boats, and airplanes.

The Telephone

Alexander Graham Bell worked at a school for the deaf. He wanted to build a machine that would transmit sound by electricity. And so he invented the telephone. When he spoke into the phone, the mouthpiece changed the vibration from the sound into an electric signal. The signal traveled along wires to the other telephone. The earpiece changed the signal back into sound.

This early telephone looks much different from the cell phones of today!

On March 10, 1876, he tried making the world's first telephone call. He called his assistant, Thomas A. Watson, to test his new invention—and it worked!

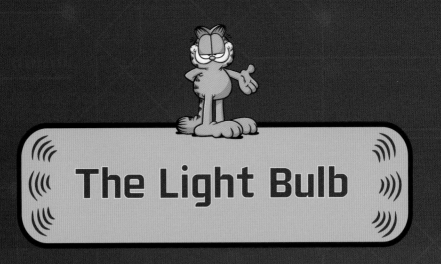

The Light Bulb

Until the nineteenth century, people burned candles for light. Scientists began trying to invent an electric light bulb. When a current of electricity passed through a carbon strip, it glowed. But the strip burned out quickly.

Thomas Alva Edison experimented with ways to improve the light bulb. He tried a strand of carbon in a bulb without oxygen. It glowed for more than forty hours. Edison eventually made a bulb that lasted more than fifteen hundred hours! With his invention, people began using electric lighting in their homes.

THAT EDISON WAS PRETTY BRIGHT!

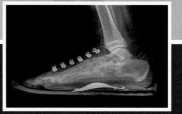

Achievements in
IGNORANCE

From the 1920s through the 1950s, US shoe stores featured the Foot-O-Scope. It was based on a machine invented by Thomas Edison. The Foot-O-Scope took X-rays to find a customer's size. But X-rays can be dangerous. The machine was phased out when people realized it wasn't a good idea to measure shoe size this way.

LUCKILY, THERE'S NOTHING IN HERE TO X-RAY

The Airplane

In 1899 Orville and Wilbur Wright experimented with how to fly. They wanted to create a flying machine. They tried to figure out how to design the wings. They watched birds closely to see how their wings worked. They took what they learned and tried to design an aircraft. Then they would fly it, observe how it worked, and refine the design. They failed many times.

IF AT FIRST YOU DON'T SUCCEED... FLY, FLY AGAIN!

Wilbur and Orville Wright's first plane takes to the air.

On December 17, 1903, they made four short flights at Kitty Hawk, North Carolina. They had invented the first powered airplane. The aerial age had begun!

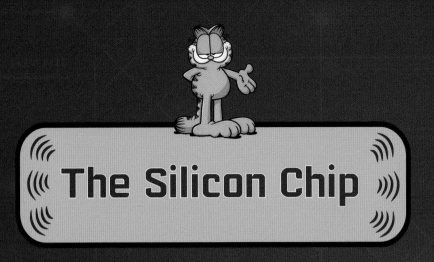

The Silicon Chip

Early computers contained vacuum tubes. These thumb-sized glass tubes relayed electrical signals inside the computer. A single computer might have eighteen thousand vacuum tubes. All those tubes made computers big and bulky.

This image shows a desktop computer's main processor.

THE CHIPS I LIKE BEST COME IN A BAG

In 1947 scientists at Bell Telephone Laboratories invented a smaller transistor for transmitting electricity. By the 1960s, thousands of transistors could be crammed onto a tiny silicon wafer, or chip. As silicon chips have gotten smaller and more powerful, so have computers. Tiny silicon chips are the heart of modern computers, tablets, and smartphones.

GPS

For centuries, sailors and explorers have searched for ways to find their position on the globe. They created detailed maps and learned to read the stars.

But in the twentieth century, the US military came up with a better way. They wanted a way to move airplanes, ships, and troops at night. In 1993 the US Air Force finished launching twenty-four satellites into orbit. The network of satellites work together for the Global Positioning System (GPS). With a GPS receiver, you can instantly learn your exact location anywhere on the planet. You'll never get lost!

Some cars include GPS systems like this one, but many people use a cell phone's GPS to navigate.

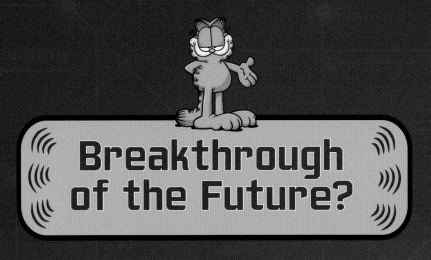

Breakthrough of the Future?

Would you like to ride in a self-driving car?

In the future, everyone could get around in cars that drive themselves. Self-driving cars already roll along the streets in many cities. You can also expect to ride buses that drive without bus drivers. You may even hop on board planes that fly without pilots.

I'M PROGRAMMING MY CAR TO GO TO EVERY DOUGHNUT SHOP IN TOWN!

PAWS-ON PROJECT

ORVILLE AND WILBUR WRIGHT TRIED DIFFERENT WAYS TO CREATE A FLYING MACHINE. Test your own skills in a contest with friends. Here's how: Have everyone fold a letter-sized sheet of paper to make an airplane. Then launch your airplanes by hand and test them in three categories. First, measure the straight-line distance from launch to landing. Next, use a watch to time how long each airplane stays in the air. Finally, test for accuracy. Aim for a target, such as a chair placed about 10 feet (3 m) from the launch site. Which designs scored best in which categories?

Glossary

combustion: a chemical process in which fuel is burned in the presence of oxygen

cylinder: a part of an engine that is hollow and shaped like a barrel

optics: the branch of science that deals with light and vision

pendulum: a hanging object that can swing freely back and forth under the action of gravity

piston: a sliding piece that moves within a hollow tube

transistor: an electronic device that controls the flow of electricity in a computer

Further Information

Hamen, Susan E. *Who Invented the Telephone? Bell vs. Meucci.* Minneapolis: Lerner Publications, 2018.

Jones, Charlotte Foltz. *Mistakes That Worked: The World's Familiar Inventions and How They Came to Be.* New York: Delacorte, 2016.

Mycielska, Malgorzata. *Impossible Inventions: Ideas That Shouldn't Work.* Gecko: Minneapolis, 2018.

National Park Service: Thomas Edison
https://www.nps.gov/edis/learn/kidsyouth/index.htm

Smithsonian National Air and Space Museum: The Wright Brothers
https://airandspace.si.edu/exhibitions/wright-brothers/online/

TED-Ed: The History of Keeping Time
https://ed.ted.com/lessons/the-history-of-keeping-time

Index

Photo Acknowledgments

Image credits: silver tiger/Shutterstock.com, pp. 2, 3, 6, 7, 10, 11, 14, 15, 22, 23, 26, 27, 30, 31; Artistdesign29/Shutterstock.com, pp. 4, 5, 8,12, 13, 16, 17, 18, 19, 20, 24, 25, 28; W. Scott McGill/Shutterstock.com, p. 5; Alexandr Shevchenko/Shutterstock.com, p. 7; Gulsahinko/Shutterstock.com, p. 9; MenchOB/Shutterstock.com, p. 11; GeorgiosArt/Getty Images, p. 13; pardon06/Shutterstock.com, p. 14; BCFC/Shutterstock.com, p. 15; Chekunov Aleksandr/Shutterstock.com, p. 17; Steve Wisbauer/Getty Images, p. 18; yumiyum/Getty Images, p. 21; Ksanawo/Shutterstock.com, p. 21; Keystone-France/Getty Images, p. 23; Fotokot197/Getty Images, p. 24; Image Source/Getty Images, p. 27; Sundry Photography/Shutterstock.com, p. 28.

Cover Images: silver tiger/Shutterstock.com; Artistdesign29/Shutterstock.com.